W9-ALW-150

Norma Simon

The Saddest Time

pictures by Jacqueline Rogers

ALBERT WHITMAN & COMPANY, MORTON GROVE, ILLINOIS

Library of Congress Cataloging-in-Publication Data

Simon, Norma.
    The saddest time.

    Summary: Explains death as the inevitable end of life and
provides three situations in which children experience
powerful emotions when someone close has died.
    1. Death—Juvenile literature. 2. Bereavement—Juvenile
literature. [1. Death] I. Rogers, Jackie, ill. II. Title.
HQ1073.3.S57   1986   155.9'37   85-15785
ISBN 0-8075-7203-9 (lib. bdg.) ISBN 0-8075-7204-7 (pbk.)

The text of this book is set in fourteen-point Janson.

Text © 1986 by Norma Simon.
Illustrations © 1986 by Jacqueline Rogers.
Published in 1986 by Albert Whitman & Company,
6340 Oakton Street, Morton Grove, Illinois 60053.
Published simultaneously in Canada by
General Publishing, Limited, Toronto.
All rights reserved. No part of this book may be reproduced or
transmitted in any form or by any means, electronic or
mechanical, including photocopying, recording, or by any
information storage and retrieval system, without permission
in writing from the publisher.
Printed in the United States of America.
10   9   8   7   6   5

For Wendy: my daughter, my teacher, my friend.

Each year, on your birthday,
people celebrate the day you were born.
They sing, "Happy birthday to you!"
They give you a cake and presents.
Everyone feels glad.
Your birth day,
the beginning of your life,
was a wonderful day in your family.

The end of life is called death.
Flowers and trees die.
Insects, fishes, birds, and animals die.
And people die, too.
When someone dies, that person is no longer alive
to talk to, to play with, to love.
When someone dies,
it is a time for feeling sad.

Michael will always remember the sad time
when his Uncle Joe was dying.

One day when Michael answered the phone,
he knew right away. Bad news.
Aunt Jane didn't say hi the way she usually did.
No, just, "Michael, please let me talk to your mother."
Michael watched Mom's face. Something was wrong.
"Yes, Jane," Mom said. "We understand.
We'll come by after supper. We love you."

Mom hung up the phone.
"Oh, Michael," she said, "you know how sick Uncle Joe's been.
For a long time the doctors have tried to help him.
But today they told Uncle Joe the terrible news
that there is nothing more they can do."

"Do you mean Uncle Joe is going to die?" Michael asked.

His mother put her arms around him.
"I'm afraid it's true," she said.
"Uncle Joe isn't going to get well,
and he is going to die pretty soon."

Michael didn't eat much supper that night.
Even chocolate pudding didn't taste good.
He couldn't believe Uncle Joe was dying.
He thought about his uncle when he used to be
healthy and strong, just like Michael's dad.
He remembered the fun
he and his cousins Paul and Hannah had
with the kites Uncle Joe made in his shop.
Uncle Joe never stopped smiling
when his kites were flying high.

After dinner, Michael and his parents went to visit Uncle Joe.
Michael felt shy. He didn't know what to say to his uncle.
But Uncle Joe looked happy to see his nephew.

"How's your basketball team?" he asked Michael.
"We're getting better," Michael said.
His uncle smiled. "I wish I could say the same."

When they got home, Michael asked his mom,
"What if this happened to us?
What if you or Dad were going to die?"
It scared Michael to talk about dying.
It scared him to even think about it.

"I know you're frightened," his mother told him,
"but don't worry about Dad or me.
Most people don't die young, like Uncle Joe.
Your dad and I are strong and healthy,
and we'll probably live to be very old."

Uncle Joe got sicker and sicker.
One day Mom said, "Uncle Joe died this morning."
Michael cried and cried,
and his mom and dad cried a lot, too.

For Aunt Jane, Paul, and Hannah,
this was the hardest time of their lives.
To help them, many people came to Uncle Joe's house.
They came to tell his family they were sorry Uncle Joe died.
Aunt Jane didn't know all the people,
but all of them knew Uncle Joe.
People came and went all day, but Uncle Joe's house
felt empty and strange because Uncle Joe was gone.

Michael wanted to help his aunt, so he fed the dog
and carried in wood for the fire.
Mom cooked and cleared the table, and Dad washed dishes.
Aunt Jane and the children sat and listened
to stories people told them about Uncle Joe.

When all the people left,
Aunt Jane thanked Michael, Mom, and Dad.
Michael hugged his aunt and cousins.

Michael wished Uncle Joe were still alive,
but he knew his wish couldn't come true.
"We can't bring Uncle Joe back," Dad said,
"but we can find ways to help his family."

Thinking about ways he could help
made Michael feel a little bit better.
"Tomorrow I'll rake their leaves," he said,
"and next spring I'll help plant their garden."

And Michael knew that whenever
he saw a high-flying kite,
he would remember his Uncle Joe.

Most people live long lives.
They see their children grow up,
and they play with their grandchildren.
But once in a while, someone dies
much too young, much too soon.
That's what everyone in Fleetwood School said
when Teddy Baker died.

The gym was quiet
the morning after Teddy Baker's accident.
Mrs. Jackson, the principal, told everyone what happened.

"Teddy rode his bike out of the driveway.
He probably didn't see the car coming down the road.
The driver couldn't stop in time, and he hit Teddy.
Teddy died in the ambulance on the way to the hospital.
His father and mother were there with him.

"Teddy Baker was only eight years old,
much too young to die.
All of us wish, with all our hearts,
that this terrible accident had never happened."

In Mr. Grady's classroom, Teddy's desk sat empty.

"Poor Teddy," said Ramona. "He must have hurt a lot."
"I never knew anyone who died before," Sarah said.

Matthew said, "I was only four when my dog died.
I thought he would be dead for just a little while.
I didn't understand he'd never be alive again."

"I wish Teddy had looked before he rode into the street,"
Charlie said. "My dad always says, 'Look both ways first.'"

"I feel awful about Teddy," David said.
"He was always pushing me in line, and yesterday
I got so mad I called him a mean name.
Now I can't tell Teddy I'm sorry for what I said."

"Of course you're very sorry," Mr. Grady said.
"When someone dies, it's natural to wish
you'd been nicer to that person.
But Teddy wasn't perfect, and neither are any of us."

"My mom is writing a letter to Teddy's folks," Jacob said.
"Could we do that, too?"

"That's a good idea, Jacob," Mr. Grady said.
He handed out paper to the class.

The children talked about what to write.
They talked about Teddy's spelling prize,
the jokes he liked to tell,

the packages of sunflower seeds he always shared,

and the great rock collection he brought to school.

The more they talked, the more they remembered.
They hoped their letters would make his mother and father
know how much they missed their friend Teddy Baker.

*It is natural for flowers to die
at the end of summer,
and it is natural for people to die
after a long life.
Emily's grandma was very sick.
She knew it was time for her to die.
She was not afraid, but she was sorry
to leave the people she loved.
And the people she loved, especially Emily,
were very sorry to say goodbye to her.*

When Emily's grandma lay dying,
her family stood by her bed.
Grandma reached out her hand to Emily.
Emily squeezed it gently.
Grandma tried hard to smile.
She wanted to cheer up her family.
But nobody felt cheerful.

Emily was very sad and a little scared, too.
The hospital room was still
when Grandma stopped breathing.
Suddenly everyone was crying,
and Emily knew that Grandma was dead.

Grandma's funeral was on a rainy day.
The church was filled with family and friends.
The minister said nice things about Emily's grandma
and the good long life she had lived.

Emily knew that Grandma had lived a long time,
but it wasn't long enough for Emily.
She felt angry.
Why did Grandma have to die?
Emily saw how old Grandpa looked,
with his wrinkled face and tired eyes.
It wasn't fair for Grandma to leave Grandpa all alone.
It wasn't fair at all!

At the cemetery,
Emily cried and cried as if her heart would break.

After the funeral, Grandpa stayed at Emily's house.
For many days, Emily and her family talked about Grandma.
Her father told Emily, "I was lucky to be part of her family.
Ever since your mother and I decided to marry,
Grandma treated me like her very own son."

Emily's mother said,
"Grandma enjoyed so many things!
Remember how she never missed her bowling?

And remember how Grandma and Emily liked to look at pictures
in Grandma's photo album, even when Emily was very small?"

Emily told her family about the oatmeal cookies
she and Grandma baked, and how they would always eat two,
hot from the oven. "Those were the tastiest cookies
in the whole wide world," Emily said.

Grandpa liked to talk about Grandma, too,
even though it sometimes made him cry.
"Talking makes me feel less alone," he told Emily.
"And talking helps keep Grandma's memory
alive and well in all the people she loved."

Talking and crying made Emily feel better, too.
After a while she didn't feel quite so sad and angry anymore.

It's been a few years since Grandma died.
Emily is older now. She still misses her grandma,
but the missing doesn't hurt as much. When she bakes
oatmeal cookies, she always eats one, hot from the oven,
and remembers Grandma with special love.

Your life is full of beginnings—
making a new friend,
learning to ride your bike,
sleeping over at a friend's house for the first time.
New and interesting beginnings
will happen all the years of your life.

But with your happy new beginnings
will be some sad times, too,
when other people's lives end,
when dying happens to people you love.

Beginnings and endings,
joy and sadness,
birth and death—
they are a part of life
for you, for everyone.

A Note About This Book

The celebration of life and the mourning of death are both part of the human experience. The modern child may have difficulty putting death in its proper perspective as a sad and sometimes tragic event but also the inevitable end of life.

This difficulty stems partly from the influence of television and movies. Here death is commonplace but elicits little genuine emotion. In cartoons, younger children see figures who were "killed" pop right up again. When older children see a murder in a movie or TV drama, adults assure them that "it's only make-believe." And as news reports of actual war, natural disasters, and accidents pass daily across the TV screen, children, like adults, learn to inure themselves to what they are seeing.

Many children grow up without ever experiencing the reality of the death of a close friend or family member. When an important person in a child's life dies, it is likely that the death takes place at a hospital, making the event remote and mysterious. Often, the experience of the death of a beloved pet provides a child's first understanding of the concept.

All children need to accept and understand death as a natural event of life. Those who must face the death of a person close to them need special help to cope with this trauma. Adults need to be sensitive to what children already know and what they need to know. Sometimes children's questions, dreams, and behavior will reflect their concerns about death, and adults can respond to these cues. At other times, grown-ups must gently bring up the subject and give the children in their care simple and honest information. A warm tone of voice and physical affection will do much to reassure the child who is trying to assimilate painful ideas. In families where religion plays a central role, children can also be helped by the explanations and comfort offered by their faith.

This book can help to stimulate dialogue between adults and children on the essential subject of life and death.

NORMA SIMON